The Battlefield of the Mind

Donald Dees

About the Author

The life of Donald (Donny) P. Dees is a story of God's infinite grace and mercy. Raised in a Christian home by Godly parents he rebelled against God at a young age. He eventually surrendered his life to the Lord at the age of 25 and entered the ministry four years later. He started as an evangelist and teacher of the Word preaching and teaching in homes, churches, on street corners, in parking lots and city parks. He held the first gospel crusade in Ghana, West Africa in many years, a country that had been closed to foreign ministers; and preached it on the same soccer field that A. A. Allen preached his last crusade in that country. He eventually moved into the prophets' office and is the original apostle and founder of True Word Ministries, Inc.

Enormous, prolonged stress led to a "fall from grace" and a short trip to federal prison for a misconstrued internet chat incident. Suffering from clinical depression and post traumatic stress disorder Donny turned his back on God for almost ten years. But the grace, mercy and faithfulness of God was able to heal his brokenness and bring him back into the sheepfold. He endeavors to continue to do a work for God through his teaching ministry by putting his knowledge, experience and revelation of the Word into print. You can listen to some of his teaching at: **https://www.true-word-ministries.org/** under the **Online Learning Resources** page.

Donny also served honorably in the United States Marine Corps Reserve, is a certified scuba diver, and holds masters rank in Korean martial arts. He currently resides in his hometown of Pascagoula, Mississippi.

Books written by Donny include:

- The Divine Flow of Authority
- New Testament Healing Scriptures
- Sermon Outlines – Vol. 1
- Manifestations of the Spirit – God's Abilities Flowing Through You
- Sermon Outlines – Vol. 2
- The Holy Spirit of God
- The Book of Exodus: A Research Paper
- Jesus of Nazareth – The Christ of God
- The Healing Power of God
- The Book of Genesis: A Research Paper
- The Angels of God
- How to Know the Voice of God – How Does God Speak to Man
- Healing – A Covenant Promise
- First Things First – Building a Solid Foundation
- After the Due Order – Apostolic Order for Prophetic Ministry

- The Dark Side Exposed – A Study in Demonology and Deliverance

Introduction

This book is the result of a short teaching that I did in my church back in 1989. I have simply reformatted the cassette tapes into digital files and transcribed them. Very little editing has been done for two reasons: first, I believe it is more effective in teaching to talk in the "street language" of the people you are addressing. Secondly it was done for the sake of expediency. You will notice a distinct "southern" accent I'm sure. I'm more concerned with getting the truth out there and made available than in spending time word-smithing.

It will no doubt be "preachy" at times. I hope this isn't a problem for you. Personally, I think we all need a little "preaching at" from time to time. It helps keep us humble and focused.

I intentionally "murder the English language" at times for the sake of levity. I hope this doesn't offend you to the point that you can't receive the truth I'm attempting to convey and instead will recognize the humor behind it.

All Scripture references are from the King James Version of the Bible unless otherwise noted. It's not that I think the King James is necessarily the best or even most accurate translation of the Bible; it is just that it is the particular version that I started with, have done the most study from, and still prefer. I encourage you to compare the Scriptures with as many translations as possible.

All underlining, bold font, etc, are added by the author for emphasis and are not part of the original texts.

Table of Contents

Chapter 1

We are in a battle. Some people say: "Well you know, the battle is the Lord's; it's not ours." Have you ever heard that? "Well you know, God's already won the war." That's exactly right. He has won the war, no doubt about it but yet we still see many skirmishes going on don't we? I mean, you don't have to be a theologian to figure out we're still fighting battles.

Don't ever let a preacher get up and tell you: "The battle's not ours; it's the Lord's bless God; so you just lay back; you don't have to worry about it. God will handle everything for you."

That's a bald face lie. It is. Goofy, pencil necked, limp wristed, hair brained preachers are destroying the people of God because they are ministering lies and error into their lives. They do nor rightly divide the Word of Truth.

II Timothy 2:15 says to:

"Study to shew thyself approved unto God, a workman that needeth not to be ashamed, rightly dividing the word of truth."

It can be wrongly divided; and they'll tell you: "Just sit back; don't worry about it." Now listen, I'm all for the "don't worry" part. But you've got to understand that if the battle is truly the Lord's, and it is; that part is true, the battle does belong to the Lord; but listen, here's the part that you miss: Where is He? He's here in me and He's in you if you belong to Him. I'm talking about God's operation in the earth. He absolutely, unequivocally will not work on planet Earth except He do it through the Church; with the exception of those rare sovereign acts as He wills. The Church is you and me.

So if the battle belongs to the Lord, there aren't any battles in heaven, the battlefield is restricted to this mud ball we call Earth. So then the battlefield is here on planet Earth, and if it belongs to the Lord, and the Lord is operating on planet Earth through the Church He is going to fight that battle through you and me. Hello? Isn't that good? It's simple isn't it?

So you are involved in this thing aren't you? You do have a part to play don't you? Amen; so let's learn and we can become effective ministers of the gospel, we can give God something to work with and through on planet Earth and we can destroy the works of the devil as we come in contact with them.

The Bible says in I John 3:8 –

"...For this purpose the Son of God was manifested, that he might destroy the works of the devil."

I hope you know that Jesus destroyed the works of the devil when He came into contact with them. He still does. We are His body. So then how does He destroy the works of the devil today on planet Earth? He does it through us. "Sickness loose him in the name of Jesus! **I** command it." "Death you cannot have this one! I refuse to allow them to die, in the name of Jesus!"

We have a part to play. The Bible says that we are workers <u>together</u> with Him (II Cor. 6:1). It's so simple. Why has the Church missed the simplicity of the gospel for so many years?

"Well you know Brother, <u>we</u> believe... Our church teaches..." You've got people that can quote you the sixteen fundamental truths of their denomination so quick it'll make your head swim; and they can't pray a headache off of anybody. Are you with me?

Now I'm not preaching against denominations. Even Israel was divided into twelve tribes. I'm preaching against error. I'm preaching against ignorance of the truth of God's Word.

So I want to talk about a battlefield; the battlefield of the mind. Let's start by looking at Genesis chapter 3.

"Now the serpent was more subtle than any beast of the field which the Lord God had made. And he said unto the woman, Yea, hath God said, Ye shall not eat of every tree of the garden?

And the woman said unto the serpent, We may eat of the fruit of the trees of the garden:

But of the fruit of the tree which is in the midst of the garden, God hath said, Ye shall not eat of it, neither shall ye touch it, lest ye die."

Now either one of two things just happened here; either in this account right here we are receiving additional information about what God literally told Adam and Eve concerning that tree; or, she has already started adding to the Word of God because when you go over there and read what God said, "that ain't in there". It goes on to say:

"And the serpent said unto the woman, Ye shall not surely die:"

See, God didn't tell them that they couldn't touch it. He told them when they ate of it that they would die, didn't He?

"...Ye shall not surely die:"

It's encouraging to me today to know that the devil doesn't do that anymore does he? He never questions the Word of God, does he? He never insults the integrity of God or God's Word, does he? Sure he does. He has never quit. We're not ignorant concerning his devices (II Cor. 2:11).

That's the only basis that he can cause you to walk in defeat is getting you off of God's Word. He's got to try and convince you to come off of it because he doesn't have the ability to pull you off. If you get off of God's Word, <u>you</u> did it.

"I don't understand Brother why God let's all

this happen to me!" I'm going to tell you "why God let's all this happen" to you. Go look in the mirror. You are your own worst enemy. "Oh but the devil made me do that." Nice try. Grow up; grow up; the devil can't **make** you do anything against your will.

God won't, do you think for one second that He's going to allow a renegade spirit to force you into something against your will? The Bible says when we sin we are drawn away of our own lusts (Jas. 1:14). It just kind of all keeps coming back home doesn't it?

We've been so quick to jump up and point our fingers in every direction at all of our problems, except for our own way; because everybody knows that "I'm" perfect. "I mean, sure I did this, but you just don't understand." "Well I know that I was criticizing Soandso yesterday about the same thing, but that's different."

The rich young ruler came to Jesus and said: "Lord, what must I do to inherit eternal life?" Jesus said: "What do the commandments say?" And Jesus quoted him the commandments. The rich young ruler told Jesus that he had kept those from his youth up at which time Jesus told him that there was just one more little thing: Sell all you have, give it to the poor and follow me.

The Bible says that rich young ruler left. He was sad because he had great possessions. He didn't really have great possessions, great possessions had him.

And then there was another man that came up and said: "Lord, what must I do?" And the Bible said about this guy: "But he, willing to justify himself..." Hello?

"But you just don't understand bless God!" Yeah I do, but it doesn't really matter if I do or I don't. Did you know that? It doesn't matter if I understand. The only thing that matters is: What are you doing with the Word?

We're going to have to grow up if we're ever going to be able to walk in victory and power and demonstrate the reality of Christ in us, the hope of glory. Wouldn't you love to see dead people raised back to life? You're not going to do it acting like a baby. You're going to learn how to rightly divide God's Word; you're going to walk in the truth; you're going to learn how to win the battle before you'll ever be able to walk it out.

The enemy came to attack God's Word. The only basis he will ever attack you in your personal life is on the Word of God. He's going to always try and pervert it, questions its' integrity, or get you to just get out of agreement with it.

The serpent came and he said: "Hath God said?" Immediately he began to cause doubt. The devil will always try to cause you to doubt what God has promised.

You read a promise like: "By His stripes we are healed" and you may say: "Well I know healing happens today because my cousin was dying of cancer and this preacher went in there and rebuked that thing in the name of Jesus, and commanded them to live; and it left and they did. So I know God heals but, this is me. Could it really be the will of God for <u>me</u> to be healed?"

Doubt; does the Word apply to me? Is the Word for me? Yes, it's for you. God is no respecter of persons (Acts 10:34). Everything that God did for anybody in the Bible; if you'll meet the same conditions you'll reap the same benefit.

So he says in verse 5:

"For God doth know that in the day ye eat thereof, then your eyes shall be opened, and ye shall be as gods, knowing good from evil.

And when the woman saw that the tree was good for food, and that it was pleasant to the eyes, and a tree to be desired to make one wise, she took of the fruit thereof, and did eat, and gave also unto her husband with her;"

Adam was not on the other side of the garden; he was sitting right there and was in open rebellion against God. So quit blaming your wife.

"...and he did eat.

And the eyes of them both were opened, and they knew that they were naked; and they sewed fig leaves together, and made themselves aprons."

Now let's go over to II Corinthians 11:3.

"But I fear, lest by any means, as the serpent beguiled Eve through his subtilty, so your <u>minds</u> should be corrupted from the simplicity that is in Christ."

Paul saw this coming to the Church 2,000 years ago. I want you to understand today that the fall of humanity occurred on the battlefield of the mind, the intellect; when man decided to leave his natural created order; when he decided that he would cease functioning according to the divine order, which is spirit.

"For as many as are led by the Spirit of God, they are the sons of God" (Rom. 8:14).

"God is a Spirit: and they that worship him must worship him in spirit and in truth" (Jn. 4:24).

God said: *"Let us make man in our image, after our likeness,"* (Gen. 1:26); and He did. Man is created as the same class of being as God Himself. Don't choke on that. If you spit it up, get you another dose of it and keep chewing.

God is Spirit; man is also a spirit being so that God can commune with him. God's divine order is that man was created to function according to his spirit. He has a soul. He lives inside of a body. So when we leave the natural order; or God's natural order which is being led of the Spirit in spite of intellect; in spite of reasoning's; we enter into an arena that we're probably going to get whipped up on.

That's exactly what caused the fall of humanity. They left the spirit realm and entered over into the soulish realm, and that's Satan's stomping grounds.

So the battlefield for the Christian is fought on the mind. This has always been the case and will be until the Lord Jesus returns and we receive our glorified bodies; and that evil one is cast into that lake that burns with fire and brimstone.

Every victory, every battle that is ever won is fought on this turf; it's fought in this arena first and foremost. Every defeat that you will ever suffer in your life; you'll lose it first in the battlefield and the arena of your mind.

I can't tell you the number of times that I have caused myself to get hurt after having heard the voice of God; after God revealing His divine will in a specific matter; rather than following that flow; following the leading of my heart I began to reason. I began to "think it through". "Ah, you know that doesn't make sense."

You should know and understand that God's thoughts are higher than our thoughts. His ways are higher than our ways (Isa. 55:9). But when I began to reason and use my intellect I'd blow it every single time. I mean every time. And over the years I've learned that when God speaks; when there's an unction or a quickening if you will, in my heart; if I'll immediately obey that I'll see victory; I'll see the power and the blessings of God released not only into my life, but into the lives of others.

I want to be a blessing to you. I want you to be a blessing to others. The Bible says that if we'll give it will be given back into our bosom, good measure, pressed down, shaken together and running over shall <u>men</u>; men will bring you blessings (Lk. 6:38).

We had a fellow, I didn't particularly know him but my wife knew him that used to come in our business. The Bible says that the wealth of the sinner is laid up for the just (Prov. 13:22). Now if you're not careful and you don't renew your mind you'll miss the blessings of God through spiritual ignorance, pride and arrogance.

This fellow brought us a sculpted piece. It was a collector's item and very expensive. This fellow who was not a Christian to my knowledge brought and gave this to my wife to fulfill the Word of God.

The Bible did not say "Christians" will bring into your bosom good measure, pressed down, shaken together and running over. And the Bible did not say when you give to another Christian God will bring back into your bosom.

We're talking about spiritual law. We give, and it goes way beyond just money. We give our life; and God honors that; and even causes rank sinners to bring and bless us. But we had to learn these things because they don't just start happening. And if you don't get yourself in a position to be able to recognize when God is moving and trying to bless you you'll send them on.

"I can't receive that." Why? Sure you can. Get your pride out of the way. Get your ignorance out of the way. Get your blindness out of the way. God's doing everything in the world to try and bless and prosper you, and you're fighting God. Why; because you're losing it in your head. You're reasoning in your mind why you shouldn't do this, or that, or why this doesn't look right to you; rather than going to the Word of God and seeing what is written.

I'm talking about growing up. We've got people in the Church that have been born of the Spirit of God, some 10, 15, 20, 25, 30, 35, 40, 45 years they've been born-again and still can't receive any blessings from God because they are spiritually blind and ignorant. They are so steeped in religiosity and in traditions of men; and in arrogance and pride that it's impossible for God to bless them.

I don't know about you but I want to be in a position where God can bless me. I've found out something; even babies can understand this: It's better to be blessed than cursed. So let's learn how to cooperate with God so that we can enjoy the blessings. And understand that they will always come with persecutions but that's no big deal because Jesus has already overcome the world.

Attitudes develop in the mind. Attitudes create. Now I want to be real clear here. I am not talking about "positive thinking". The Bible has never taught "positive thinking". There are people who have taught "positive thinking" and have gone in and pulled pieces of the Bible out and put in their books, and tried to justify their teaching.

Jesus never taught "positive thinking". The Bible teaches "right thinking". What is right thinking? It is thinking the way that God thinks. He's always right. Did you know that the Bible is actually the thoughts of God? They came out of His mind. The Bible came out of the mind of God therefore it's God's thoughts. We can think God's thoughts; and that's right thinking; and right thinking produces right speaking and right acting; and that brings victory.

But wrong thinking produces wrong talking, and wrong actions; and that always brings defeat; every time. It's so simple it's almost scary. And yet, the majority of the Church world has never grasped it. If they have they're in rebellion because they won't use it.

So, we study these things, and rehearse these things, and remind ourselves of these things, lest any promise that's been given unto us; we'd miss it; it would slip. So we want to understand that the mind of man has to be dealt with. It's very crucial to your victory or the quality of life that you'll live while you're in the here and now.

Oh we'll have it made on the other side. That's not what our worry is, is it? It's: What kind of quality of life do you have in the here and now?

"Well you know Brother; we believe that God doesn't want His people to have all of the finer things of life. God doesn't want His people having nice homes you know; He's more concerned with feeding the poor."

Why then did Jesus say: You're always going to have the poor with you; take that expensive oil and pour it on my feet? Why do you reckon Jesus wears a big ole band of gold around His waist? Why do you reckon if God doesn't want His people blessed He's given me gold rings, and diamonds, and necklaces, and bracelets? I didn't buy any of them. God blessed me with it. God gave it to me through somebody else.

God wants you blessed. We tell people: God loves you. "Why am I starving to death? Why am I dying with AIDS? Why am I dying with cancer if God's so good? How come you're wearing blue jeans with holes all in them? Don't God love you too?"

Well, sure He loves me. "Well didn't you

21

just tell me God can do anything?" Sure I did. "Well, can't He get you some clothes that look half way decent? You want to preach this to me and you ain't walkin in it?"

That's straight shooting isn't it? It's getting where you live. You have to apply it to where you live or it doesn't do you any good.

God wants you blessed. I'm not saying that God wants you to have a 15 million dollar house. I'm not preaching that junk. That's extremism; that's fanaticism; that's goofy stuff. But you ought to be able to enjoy the things that God has provided. He built this thing for you and me. He didn't build it for the devil. He didn't make this mud ball and put all of the gold, and silver, and precious stones and jewels in it for the devil. He put it here for you and me. So let's quit being goofy about it in our thinking.

Chapter 2

In the last chapter I established the fact that the battlefield for the Christian is not in his spirit. In Mark 11:23 Jesus said:

"For verily I say unto you, That whosoever shall say unto this mountain, Be thou removed, and be thou cast into the sea; and shall not doubt in his heart, but shall believe that those things which he saith shall come to pass; he shall have whatsoever he saith."

Notice He only said the word "believe" one time in that Scripture; and He mentioned the word "say" or "saith" three times. Do you reckon that was a coincidence? I don't think so. You see, the problem is not with believing in our heart. We read the Word of God; we see it; we know it; we have the witness of the Spirit when we see the good promises of God; that anointing on the inside; you just want to jump out of your body.

You know, you're reading the Word of God and you come across a promise, and BOOM; it jumps off the page and hits you right between the eyes; that rhema comes alive; quickened by the Holy Spirit. Hallelujah.

You don't have any problem believing that on the inside do you? The problem is not with our spirit man believing the promises of God.

I would hope you know there is an enemy;

he's alive; he's not very well but he is alive; he's roaming the earth; he's looking for people that he can destroy and devour. You've got to be a willing volunteer for him to do that. But do you know what; you'll be destroyed without the knowledge of God because Hosea said:

"My people are destroyed for lack of knowledge:" (Vs. 6a).

That doesn't mean that you have to jump up and go get you a college degree. I'm not against college degrees; I'm for them. That's not the kind of knowledge he's talking about. He's talking about knowledge of God's methods, means and motives; God's Word, His will and His way. How does God function? How does God flow? How will God reveal Himself? How do I get plugged in to that?

That's it in a nutshell. How do I take the knowledge of God's Word; how do I take the anointing of God and make it work on my job? How do I make it work in my family? How do I effectively enter into combat with my enemy and subdue him, dominate him and repel him?

He's real; and all you've got to do is to pick up the newspaper to see how active he is; to see his works. And you are engaged; listen to me now, whether you like it or not is irrelevant; it's not even required for you to like it. You don't have to like this; it's not a requirement. It's a simple matter of fact. You are in a war.

"I don't want to be!" Too bad. It's not optional. You have an enemy. He's constantly waging war against you. He's trying to steal, kill and destroy your life. And any little bitty facet of your life that you let your guard down in he's going to slip a hook in. Amen; he'll knock you down; he'll knock you out; he'll kick your teeth in. Don't think that he's going to be a gentleman when he knocks you down and back off and say: "Well go ahead and get up. I'll wait. Come on."

He'll stomp your guts out. He hates you. He despises you! All he wants to do is mock God through you. So knowing these things it behooves us to wise up and grow up; get ready to go up. But until we do we need to learn how to "occupy". You know that's a military term too. Anytime when they talk on the news about Israel they'll talk about the "occupied territory". That's ridiculous because the Jews own Israel and have for thousands of years; but that's another story.

We have been put on this earth to occupy. We are to destroy the works of the devil as we come in contact with them. We are to dispossess the inhabitants of this land. This land is filled with giants. And you can either be a grasshopper in your own eyes; or you can be a Joshua generation child of God that says: "We are well able because their defence has departed from them."

You see, the enemies defence has departed

from him, but he'll try and convince you it hasn't. And if you do not have the knowledge of God's Word and who you are <u>in Him</u> he'll deceive you. He is the great deceiver.

So you see the battlefield for the Christian is really not in his heart. He's got to win the victory, or suffer his loss and defeat in the battlefield of the mind.

I showed you that the fall of mankind did not happen in the realm of the spirit. It happened when woman, Eve, left her spiritual realm and entered into a realm of intellectualism if you will; the mind, the soul. Satan operates primarily through the soulish and the physical realm against you. And your mind is in your soul, it's not part of your spirit; it's not part of your body. Your brain is not your mind. It's your brain. It is the physical part of you that the invisible part of the soul uses to manifest itself through if you will.

If you stepped outside of your body you wouldn't know it. You'd still think the same way you're thinking right now. You'd still see; you'd still hear. The only thing that you couldn't do is make contact with me or anyone else. You could touch me but I wouldn't be able to feel you. You could not make contact with me. That's why you have a body. The body, *soma*, slave, was given to you so that you could express yourself on planet Earth; and the brain is the instrument that the soul expresses itself through.

So you have to understand that the enemy is going to try and deceive you, to seduce you, trip you up by operating in the soulish and the physical. As surely as you are tempted in the mind, a thought is shot in: Bloom! That's a temptation. You are standing at a crossroad. You've got to do something one way or the other. That's how he'll tempt you in your soulish realm.

What about the body? "Oh God, help me God. I think I'm having a heart attack." That pain is real isn't it? It feels real anyway. It hurts. You start getting that numbness, and burning, and shortness of breath. "I'm dying, I'm dying, I'm dying!"

That is one of two things. Either you really are having a heart attack; or, the devil's trying to convince you to have one because he is able to cause pain to appear in your physical body. Many times I have had sharp pains, deep pains in my heart. And I've immediately heard a lie that said: "You're about to have a heart attack." Now that's happened to me just time, and time, and time again.

And immediately a battle would begin. Do you know what? You don't have to be sick to die and you don't have to be old and not sick to die. You have the ability with the faith of God inside you to end your life without ever lifting a hand against yourself.

I'm not talking about committing suicide. I'm talking about: Lose the will to live. I know a man that almost did it one time. God sent three different prophets to him before he turned the thing around. He was dying and the doctors couldn't find anything physically wrong with him.

He was so fed up, so hurt that all he wanted to do was go home. He was on his way. And God sent three different prophets; one right behind the other. One called him from across the nation, from California; and he had a couple of others get a hold of him; and they ministered the Word of God to him; and BOOM; it broke that thing for him.

The battlefield is in the mind saint. Your spirit is filled with the Spirit of God. There are denominations that teach Christians can't have demons (see my book *The Dark Side Exposed – A Study in Demonology and Deliverance*). I came out of one that teaches that and believes that. They'll crucify you for even talking that way. By the way I believe that particular denomination just happens to be the greatest persecutor of the Prophetical Restoration Movement of any other Pentecostal or Charismatic group. They stand head and shoulders above the others.

At any rate, they'll teach you: "There is no way a Christian can have a demon." I beg to differ. I'll say this: If you're truly born of the Spirit of God the Holy Spirit is in your spirit. You don't have a demon in your spirit until you blaspheme the Holy Spirit. Did you know that you can't blaspheme the Holy Spirit unless you're born-again? Sinners can't do it and I can show you in the Word (Heb. 6:4-6).

You've got to be born-again before you can even blaspheme the Holy Spirit. Now that kind of shoots holes all in that ole "Once Saved Always Saved" junk doesn't it? I'm not attacking denominations. I'm not calling any groups' name. I'm attacking the spirit of error and false doctrine.

But you see you've got to understand that you are more than a spirit being; you have a soul, and you're walking around inside of a body. And there are certain sicknesses that are the direct result of a demon spirit who has literally latched on to a physical body, and he's choking that part of the body.

Not all, but much of cancer is this way. That's why you can pray for people for healing until your tongue falls out, you can turn black and blue, you wear your knees out: "Heal em God; heal em God; heal em" and they die. They didn't need to be healed. They needed a demon spirit to be dealt with.

The life of your body is the spirit inside the body. Isn't that right? When that spirit man steps outside of that body it's going to the ground; it's dropping. You're just going to keep right on truckin. You're either going up or you're going down; you're not going to a holding tank. You're going up or you're going down. Paul said to be absent from the body is to be present with the Lord (II Cor. 5:8). Jesus told about the rich man and the poor man. He said when that rich man died where did he go; Purgatory; uh ah; he went to hell.

Did you know you can't find the word "Purgatory" anywhere in the Bible; nowhere; Old or New Testament? You can't even find any hint of a place called Purgatory.

He went to a place of torment; a place of flames called hell. And in hell he lifted up his eyes, and said: "Father Abraham let Lazarus..." You know the story.

So many times you can have for example, someone who has cancer and the life of that cancer is a spirit. And when the spirit comes out of the flesh it dies (the cancer). Why do you think the Bible says lay hands suddenly on no man? Have you ever wondered about that? He's not talking about giving somebody five; although that may be included in there. Why do you think it says that?

You've got to have the mind of God to know how to pray; what to deal with. Now here's a good general rule when you're praying for sick people: Always pray for healing <u>unless</u> the Spirit of God reveals to you that there is spirit activity.

"How's He going to do that?" He'll do it through the word of knowledge or discerning of spirits; or even through prophecy. "Well we don't think we need all that." Well you just go on and live that ole pitiful, poor, defeated and dejected life that you're living. You must know more than God knows with that kind of attitude because He thought you did need it. He thought you needed it so much that He killed His Son to purchase it.

God help us to open our eyes to the truth. Quit fighting God. God's done everything in the world to try and bless us, and minister the life of God to us; and we constantly reject it and fight tooth, hair and nail: "Uh uh, uh uh; bless God I don't believe it that way. I don't believe it that way. I don't see it that way."

Do you know what the Bible also says over in I Corinthians 14:38? If a man wants to be ignorant, let him be ignorant.

"Well I'm going to stay over here Brother and I'm going to convert my church. I'm going to change my denomination." Yeah, right. Sure you are; you and the 14 jillion other people who went before you and said the same thing and didn't change anything.

They're that way because they chose to be that way, they want to be that way, and you're not going to change them. So get up and get in a group with those of like precious faith; those that you can work with; those that you can flow with; those that you can walk in unity and be a functioning part with and get up and go on. Don't wait for angels to come down and blow a big trumpet, and roll out a scroll, and say: "Thus says the Lord". Sometimes we get so spiritually minded that we get goofy. Amen? You know live chicks won't sit under a dead hen. And they don't need God to come tell them: "You can get out from underneath that dead hen."

Well, let me try and teach a little bit. That was my introduction to this chapter.

Now faith will work in your heart with doubt coming into your mind; but that doubt has to be properly dealt with or it will eventually choke your faith down.

Let's read Romans 12:1-2.

"I beseech you..."

Do you know what that word "beseech" means? I looked it up in the Greek; it means: beg. He's begging. Who's he? "Well Paul wrote the epistle to the Romans." Wrong. The Spirit of God wrote this thing. He just used Paul to ink it.

So when you think of it in light of that, what you're reading is: God is begging. Whew! Man that adds a whole new dimension to it doesn't it?

"...by the mercies of God, that ye present your bodies a living sacrifice, holy, acceptable unto God, which is *your reasonable service.*

*And be not conformed to this world: but be **ye** transformed by the renewing of your mind, that ye may **prove** what is that good, and acceptable, and perfect, will of God."*

"Well you know Brother we just can't ever really know what God wants." "Father if it be thy will..." Oh, barf. Don't that make you want to fill up a barf bag? You talk about a cop out. The Word of God says that I can prove what's God's good will, His acceptable will, His perfect will.

God has got a perfect will for every person. God will also let you do a lot of things and if you're not careful, if you're not renewed in your mind you'll conform to the way the world thinks.

I had a couple that left my ministry that it was abundantly clear that God didn't want them to. And I felt obligated as their pastor and as one of the prophets that had ministered into their lives to remind them of the things that God had been sharing with them; things that they themselves had testified with their mouth. Do you know what they said?

"Well Brother, we've been going and we've been holding meetings; and we've been seeing people healed; and we've been seeing miracles. Now that must mean we're in the will of God."

Ooh; man, I got creepy crawlies when I heard that. They didn't understand that God is going to honor His Word even if a jackass speaks it. Yeah; if a jackass speaks it He's going to honor His Word because He has exalted His Word and magnified His Word even above His Name.

God's going to honor your faith even if I'm in abject sin; if I'm living in adultery I can stand behind the platform and preach God's Word, and if you've got faith you'll get healed. That's a fact. He's not honoring my faith; He's honoring yours' and He's honoring His Word.

You cannot use signs, wonders and miracles as a gauge for saying: "I'm in the perfect will of God because these things are happening."

These people are no doubt in the acceptable will of God. He is allowing them to do this because we're free moral agents aren't we? He'll allow you to do all kind of things but just because you're seeing the anointing flow is no indicator you're in God's <u>perfect</u> will.

You've going to have to get your mind renewed before you can prove what will you're in. That word "renewed" in the Greek actually means: renovation.

"*Do not be conformed to this world*"; what did he mean by that? He's talking specifically about the way we think.

"*...but be ye transformed* by *the* renovation *of your mind, that ye may **prove** what is that good, and acceptable, and perfect, will of God.*"

You're going to have to renovate the way that you think when you get born-again. Now I want to show you something from James 1.

"Wherefore lay apart all filthiness and superfluity of naughtiness, and receive with meekness the engrafted word, which is able to save your souls" (Vs. 21).

Now look at verse 2.

"My brethren,"

Who is he writing to? He's writing to born-again people. Why did he tell born-again people their souls weren't saved?

There's a term that I heard all my life. I mean every since I've been in church and around church people we'd pray: "Oh God, save their souls." We're trying to get the cart before the horse aren't we? Your soul doesn't get saved, or renewed, until after the new birth.

When you received Jesus Christ as your Savior you didn't get a new body. God didn't save your body. I've got news for you: He didn't save your soul either. He didn't touch your soul. He recreated the human spirit only. The spirit man has become a new creation, a new species. You still think basically the same way you always thought. You still think defeat; you still think lack, doubt, sickness.

"Boy I heard that flu's goin around. I get it every year. I guess I'll be one of the first ones to get it." Hello? That's taking the faith of God and exercising it for negative things. Why would you do that? Do you want me to tell you why? It's because the soul, the mind has to be renovated. It has to be renewed; and it doesn't happen overnight.

It's a process. So we see that the soul of man is not what is dealt with at the new birth. You see a lot of people that maybe they're sick, and when God saves them He heals them at the same time. But they still have the same body. It's just been healed by the power of God.

So you have to deal with the area of your mind, the way that you think; and you have to transform; or let me say it this way: You have to retrain your thinking process. What you have to do is to literally learn: How does God think?

"Now, I see my check book is empty. I see this stack of bills. Hmmm. I see all these late notices. You know, bankruptcy looks pretty good."

That's the way the world thinks. And the lawyers get on the television: "For just $400..." You probably know four or five people that have filed bankruptcy. I'm not condemning anyone who has filed bankruptcy. I'm saying there is a better way. There's a better way.

But you have to renew the thinking process. You can't think about bankruptcy. But it's hard for you not to think of bankruptcy if you haven't <u>saturated yourself</u> with God's Word.

"Well you know Brother; I go to church every time the doors open." That's great. Hallelujah; you need to. You're at least doing as much as the devil does. Did he say that? Yes he did. Yeah; you're at least on the same attendance level as the devil. Aren't you proud?

It's good. It's proper. It's biblical. It's scriptural.

"Not forsaking the assembling of ourselves together, as the manner of some is; but exhorting one another: *and so much the more, as ye see the day approaching"* (Heb. 10:25).

We see the day approaching don't we? Man, we ought to never miss church. If there's any way to be there, bless God we ought to be there but that "ain't enough" beloved. I wished it were but it's not. No preacher can give you in the short time they have to deal with you what it's going to take to put you over in life. They can get you in the direction. They can plant and sow some seed. But it's up to you as to what you do with them.

You're the one that is going to have to water that seed. If you went out and stuck a seed in the earth and saw to it that it never got water it's not coming up. It is not going to grow. It is not going to bear fruit.

The Word of God is identically the same. When it's sown it must be watered. And you've got to keep those weed seeds from choking it because the enemy will come to sow weed seeds; and if you let them get down in your heart and take root it's going to choke the Word of God and it's not going to bear fruit.

But you are not born-again in your soul. You are not born-again in your mind. You are born-again in your spirit only, and at that point in time you <u>must</u> begin to rejuvenate, renovate, renew, retrain your thinking processes so that you no longer think as a mere man because you are no longer a mere man thank God. We're new creations. We're sons and daughters of God. We are a supernatural breed if you will.

But you're going to have to learn how God thinks so that you can think the way God thinks; so that you'll talk the way God talks and you'll act the way God acts. The writer said: "Be imitators of God" as dear children (Eph. 5:1 NIV).

We're going to have to imitate God hook, line and sinker, rod and reel; from A to Z. Instead of saying: "Oh God, it looks like I'm gonna die. Oh, God, it looks like I'm gonna have to go bankrupt. Oh God, it looks like I'm losin everything." We're going to have to say: "Let there be an abundance!" And it's got to come from your heart. And when those doubts, and those worries, and those fears and everything else come along we can't go: "It ain't working; it ain't working. See there it got worse."

That's the biggest sign that it's working.

That is the biggest indicator: "This thing is working bless God. I'm getting it right!" The Word says that when the seed is sown immediately the enemy comes (Mk. 4:15). If the enemy isn't coming there must not be any seed.

So we learn to live by faith and not by sight. We learn to control our thoughts. But first we renew our mind. We retrain ourselves to think God's Word first and to speak that Word; and then to start acting like it has already happened.

We believe it; we think it; we declare it; we act on it; and then our eyes behold it. So quit reversing the process. Quit saying: "When I see it I'll believe it; when I can get this sign or that sign." That's total unbelief.

"Well you know Gideon laid a fleece before God." If you try it you'll get fleeced. Laying a fleece before God is totally unscriptural for New Testament believers. You can't find anywhere in the New Testament where there were ever any fleeces laid; never, never, never.

Jesus never said: "Lay a fleece before the Father and He will confirm it." You've got the Holy Spirit of God on the inside. You've got the Holy Ghost. Jesus said through Paul: *"...as many as are led by the Spirit of God, they are the sons of God"* (Rom. 8:14). Hallelujah.

So let's get our minds renewed with God's Word. Let's make a commitment to double up.

Let's make a commitment to go evaluate our time, our activities. Let's make a commitment to examine our priorities. Some people always have time to read the newspaper but they can't ever read God's Word. Something's wrong. Something's horribly wrong.

Those people will read the newspaper and then they'll sit down for 30 minutes to an hour, and turn on the television, and listen to the same news that they just read; but they don't have time to read God's Word. And they can't figure out why their homes are being destroyed. They can't figure out why their children are running wild in the streets. Dear God help us.

There aren't any of us that have perfect children; none of us. None of us were perfect children. There's no such thing as a perfect child. I don't care how you think you've got your act together you're not going to produce a perfect child; but you're responsible to try. You are responsible and accountable to God to try.

You do your best. Live what you preach. Live what you testify to them. When you miss it go to them parents; go to them and say: "I'm sorry. I missed it. I handled that wrong. I treated you unjustly. Please forgive me." Be big enough to do that. You're their role model. You're their example.

Nothing grieves me more than to hear a young person say: "Hump. I'll never apologize.

You'll never catch me apologizing." They perceive that as a sign of weakness because we don't do it. It's time to quit playing games Church. It's time to grow up. It's time to open our eyes. Grow up; study up; pray up; and get ready to go up. Amen?

Chapter 3

Let's link a few things together and do a review. The true God kind of faith is a force; a power, an issue if you will; a well spring some translations put it, that comes out of the <u>heart</u> of man. It's placed in the heart and it issues forth from the heart. However, you must understand that man is a triune being. He is a spirit who has a soul; and the soul is the seat of mans' emotions, and mans' will, and mans' mind.

Your thought life is the most predominate; that, and then probably the emotions. Do you realize that thoughts create emotions? Thoughts can also change emotions. I'm going to show you in the Greek in a minute something that is neat about thoughts; about your mind.

See, because you're a spirit being God gave you a soul and He placed you, or set you inside of a body, a vehicle if you will, to move around in, and to express yourself in the physical world. You've got to understand that your spirit will operate from the inside; will communicate through the soul.

You should have heard the voice of your spirit at times. You should have also heard the voice of the Holy Spirit at times. That came through your mind. It issued up out of your heart into your mind.

So you see that it's crucial that we understand about spirit, soul, and body; and about the mechanical, if you will, aspects: How does faith work; so that we can understand this force, this power and we can channel it.

You know you can take a stick of dynamite and put it on top of the earth; just lay it flat on the ground and light it; and back away from it; and it will blow up and it'll make a lot of noise; and it'll throw some pebbles and some dirt but it doesn't really accomplish much. But you take that same piece of dynamite and cover it up with just a little bit of earth. You don't have to stick it six foot under; just a little bit of earth and you look at the crater it forms. Why; because you're taking the same power and focusing it.

One of the first things you learn in martial arts, or I guess in any fighting sport whether it be boxing, or karate, or whatever, is that if I take and slap you with an open hand it'll sting; it'll certainly get your attention but it's not going to do any damage. About the most I can hope for is first of all, I'm going to make you very angry with me. Amen? Do you love to get slapped in the face? I'll probably discolour the surface of the skin a little bit. And at best maybe I can get you to bite your lip and might get a few drops of blood from that. But I mean, let's face it; that isn't much damage is it?

But if I took the same amount of force delivered at the same speed, but let's say this time I took a thumb knuckle and I put that thumb inside of your temple; with the same force and the same speed. At a minimum I'd knock you out; and I stand a good chance of doing much greater damage.

Do you see what I'm getting at? Faith is power and for too long we've just set that stick of faith dynamite on top of the earth and lit the fuse; and couldn't understand why the job wasn't getting done. But see, God is giving us the Spirit of Wisdom, and revelation in the knowledge of Him. He is a faith God. And now we're studying how to focus that power and accomplish great things for God.

Amen; and on the Christians battlefield most of the time his power is diffused. After it is issued forth out of his heart he allows the enemy to diffuse that power in his mind; the battlefield of the mind.

In the last chapter I established the fact that the mind when a person is born-again must be renovated. You remember that word "renewed" in the Greek literally means to renovate. It has to be renewed; it has to be, the Scripture said it needed to be washed out. Washed out, by the washing of water, by the Word (Eph. 5:26). The Word of Almighty God is what is given to us to renovate our thinking; to revolutionize if you will our thinking.

Literally the Word of God is a collection of God thoughts. Think about it. It is a collection of God thoughts. The Word of God came from the mind of God. It is exactly how God thinks. Now get a hold of this. I know this is basic but for the most part most of us aren't moving fully in the basics yet.

You don't have to wonder how God thinks. He gave you that knowledge. The key is training ourselves to think God thoughts; being imitators of God as dear children. If I'm going to act like you I'm going to have to know how you think. You know you can spend enough time with a husband; or with a wife; or with your children and they pretty well learn you; your methods, and habits, and things so much they know how you think about certain things. They know it because they've been with you so much. Well that's what I'm talking about here; renewing the mind. You have to renew the mind and you have to maintain. It is a never ending process because I'll tell you this: You'll find that you can get yourself renewed and then just say: "Well I've got it. Hallelujah. Thank ya Lord. I, I've got it. I no longer think the way I used to about this. I think the way you think now"; boy you're strong. You've got the Word in you. And I mean the devil can hardly get within a mile of you and you smell him; and the Word begins to come out because "you've arrived".

And there's so many things you need to do. "Well you know it wouldn't hurt to not pray so long today. I don't guess I really need to read my Bible today; I can skip it today. I mean now I'm renewed. I know a lot of Scriptures. I can quote a lot of em. Look at my stack of 3 X 5 index cards from all the verses I've memorized." You do have 3 X 5 cards don't you; by subject? I'm just throwing out some little ideas for you.

If you want God to bless your finances you're going to have to start thinking like God thinks about money. Do you want God to bless your business? You're going to have to learn how God thinks about operating business; and then look at what you've been doing; and then fall on your face and thank God for His grace. Do you want to walk in divine health? Boy there's a lot of areas there you're going to have to control; starting with your big mouth. Amen; my big mouth too.

But you can never control these areas of your life without renewing your thinking process. You have to retrain your thinking process because it is your thinking process that got you in that mess. You are a product, right now; look at your life right now; you created it! You did it by the way you trained yourself to think; and you started talking what you were thinking and that produced a corresponding action which created the situation you're in right now.

But here's the good news: If you don't like where you are you don't have to stay there. Thank God for Jesus, you can renew your mind and change any situation that you're in. But it doesn't come easy; it doesn't come quick, and it doesn't happen automatically.

Let's look at I Timothy 1:7.

"For God hath not given us the spirit of fear; **_but_**..."

What is the word "but"? It's a conjunction isn't it? What do conjunctions do? They connect words and thoughts. So, what that word is doing is connecting the bottom part; or the last portion of this Scripture to the first part of it. You may say: "Why'd you give me an English lesson?" Because, what is the subject of the first part of the verse? Spirit; he's talking about a particular spirit.

"...God hath not given us..." the Church. *"...the spirit of fear; but..."* You could say it this way: *"...but* He has given us the Spirit *of power, and of love, and of a sound mind."*

That word "sound" in the Greek is **sōphrŏnismŏs** (so-fron-is-mos')[i]. It means: discipline, self control. People say: "Brother you just can't control your mind." That's not what the Word of God said. As a matter of fact, the Word of God says that God has given us a Spirit.

Who is that? It's the Holy Spirit of God, who is the power of God. He is the creative power of God and He's inside of you and me; and the creative power of God is available to enable us to discipline and control our minds.

The Word of God also says that I can do all things through Christ who strengthens me (Phil. 4:13). It is the Spirit of Christ in me, the Holy Ghost, who gives me the ability to renew my mind to the thoughts of God and control anything to the contrary.

The key is seen in Isaiah 26:3.

"Thou wilt keep him *in perfect peace,* whose *mind is stayed* on thee: *because he trusteth in thee."*

Now let me ask you this: Why would God tell you that He'd keep your mind in perfect peace if you would keep your mind stayed on Him **if** you did not have the ability to control your mind to keep it stayed on Him? Is God unjust that He would command us to do a thing that He knows we're not able to do? Certainly not; He is a just God. He's just in all of His dealings with man.

But here's what you have to understand: The Church has got this idea that we're "Oh, poor pitiful me. I'm just a helpless grub worm down here on the earth. I can't do anything." That's a lie. The devil sold you that bill of goods and you bought it. You let the devil deceive you. You're not some ole poor pitiful little grub worm. You're not some little ole helpless thing down here that can't do anything.

"Boy I'll tell you if it wasn't for God." That's right if it wasn't for God none of us would have ever been able to come forth and be here because the devil would have wiped out humanity about four thousand, five thousand years ago. Amen; but we're not helpless. God didn't leave us helpless down here. He made, I'm going to say it; it may choke you to death but if it does we'll get you resurrected; God is a God of resurrection; God made you through Jesus; through Jesus He made you a little god.

Jesus called them that. He said: *"Is it not written in your law, I said, Ye are gods"* (Jn. 10:34)? Little "g". Are you even beginning to glimpse just a little, teeny portion of what I'm trying to convey to you about the power and the ability of God that's available to every single one of us; from the littlest one up to the biggest? You don't just have to be preachers. That Scripture that talks about how beautiful are the feet of those that preach the gospel of peace **and** bring good tidings; aren't you able to preach peace; aren't you able to bring good tidings? Well then it's not just limited, is it? Hallelujah.

So we see that the power of God has been given to us, but God requires us to do it; and this is why the mental institutions are full today with people who at one time had relationship with Jesus. You see what happened was the enemy came on the battlefield of their minds and they would not keep their minds stayed on Him.

Maybe he got to some of them before they renewed their minds. And rather than going to godly men and women, and seeking the council of the elders, and allowing them to minister God's Word and deliverance into their lives, they entered into the battlefield of the mind under their own strength. And the same thing will happen to you and me that happened to Adam and Eve if we try and enter into an intellectual warfare with the enemy. We will fall. He'll win.

But if we'll keep it a spiritual battle and speak back to him the thoughts of God, because now we know how to think like God see because we've renewed our minds, there is absolutely no way he can trip us up and keep us down. You're not promised that you won't ever get knocked down. You're just promised you don't have to stay there; you can always get up.

I was reading the Proverbs one day, re-reading them, and was finishing up and there was a Proverb in there about a man that fell seven times and got up again. He fell seven times but he got up again. He fell seven; got up eight. The Proverbs of Solomon. The wisdom of God revealed to him.

You see, you'll get knocked down; you just don't have to stay there, unless you want to. And people lose that warfare because they let the devil destroy them in their minds; and fear comes in and takes hold. The book of I John says that fear has torment.

Have you ever seen somebody, or talked with somebody, or tried to minister to somebody that was in a mental institution? Those people are tormented. Have you ever been to your local hospital in the psychiatric wing and talked with people who were having nervous breakdowns? They're tormented; totally, completely tormented; dominated by fear.

But greater is He that is in us Church than he that is in the world. Jesus said in Luke 21:19:

"In your patience possess ye your souls."

Let's restructure that sentence from the

Elizabethan English, bring it to American English, modern day, just to make it a little bit clearer to our thoughts. "You"; hold up your hand and say "Me". Alright: "You patiently possess, keep control of your soul."

Did you notice that the action was not on the part of God? Religious teaching will tell you: "You can't do anything. The battle is the Lord's it's not ours Brother." But what religion doesn't tell you is that God will fight that war through you; but the Word tells you that.

The responsibility of keeping your soul, your mind, and your emotions is not up to God. Don't waste your time and God's, and your breath asking God to control your anger. He's not going to do it. He absolutely is not going to do it. He gave you a Spirit, the Holy Spirit of God to enable YOU to control your anger. And it's not a sin to be angry. Hello? Are you there?

"Be ye angry and sin not: let not the sun go down upon your wrath:" (Eph. 4:26).

Getting mad isn't wrong. God gets mad. Don't you ever think that He doesn't. The only thing that keeps His wrath from annihilating us is the fact that the blood of Jesus was shed. And when His anger rises up now Jesus says: "Remember the blood Father; remember the blood."

So, we can control our emotions. How? We change them. Do you know what I used to do when I was lost and undone without God? When I got mad I went into a rage; and if there wasn't somebody there that I could hit I'd find something to hit. I'd bust holes in walls. I'd beat my knuckles until the blood was just pouring off my hands on Stop signs, or anything. I mean just an absolute lunatic fool; absolutely no control whatsoever over my emotions. Thank God I don't do that anymore. Amen; I've learned that I do have some control.

I'll tell you what else too; I've proven this before I got saved. In one way I did it intentionally, but I wasn't trying to prove the Word of God by any stretch of the imagination; I didn't know anything about the Word of God. Everything that I'd ever been taught or learned as a child had been robbed through sin; but when I went to boot camp I found out that although my mind was constantly being attacked; see I went to a little place off the coast of South Carolina (Parris Island) and it was physically tough, but that wasn't the toughest part of boot camp. Really I guess that was about the easiest part, the physical part.

We'd go sixteen hours a day from can to can't physically. But that was probably the easiest part of boot camp. The toughest part was the mental and emotional torture that we were subjected to constantly. They literally were trying to drive us insane; and that's a fact. You may say: "Well they ought not to do that." Let me tell you why they were doing it. They had a purpose. They weren't just being mean although they were very mean. They had a purpose. If you're going to "lose it" they want you to lose it at home instead of out there in the middle of a battlefield where peoples' lives depend on how you're going to act.

I watched them one night drive a man absolutely loony. It's not a pretty sight. The devil is doing everything in his power to do the same thing to you and me. And he's using the same tactics they were using. He's attacking you mentally and he's attacking you emotionally; and he's trying to break you down in that area because he knows that if he can succeed it will overpower your spirit. Thus he has rendered you totally ineffective. He has taken a soldier of God Almighty; he's taken him out.

We're in a war. We are in a war and our success in life and the very eternal destination of some people depends on how effective we become on planet Earth. So we thank God that He's revealing these things to us so that we are able to take authority and dominion over our own life; and teach this way; they used to call Christianity: "The Way". As a matter of fact, if you go back and read the book of Acts you'll see it referred to as "the way". I like that. Don't you?

It really is the only way to live your life. And oh by the way, it just happens to be the highest quality of life that any created being can enjoy. Jesus said: *"The thief cometh not but for to steal, and to kill, and to destroy: I am come that they might have life, and that they might have* it *more abundantly"* (Jn. 10:10).

There is no more abundant life available than the Christian life; The Way; the way of God; functioning on planet Earth just like God functions.

The action is upon our part. We must initiate the action first. James 4:7 says: *"Submit yourselves therefore unto God. Resist the devil, and he will flee from you."* Most people misquote that Scripture in that they only tell you the last part of it.

"Resist the devil bless God; and he'll flee." Don't

you count on it. Don't you count on it unless you're ready to submit yourself to God first. I had a demon spirit show up at my house one night. I'd been in prayer for about an hour, an hour and a half I guess; and had gotten up and was making my way to bed when all of a sudden all of the hair on my body stood up. It stopped me dead in my tracks. I looked at my arms and they had huge goose bumps all over them. Every hair on my body was standing straight up. And this tremendous fear tried to grip me and take control.

And I said: "Dear God. What's wrong?" There was no reason for that to happen. I didn't hear anything. I didn't see anything. It was like you took a bucket of that stuff and just poured it on me; and I said: "Dear God. What's wrong?" And the Spirit of God said: "There is a demon spirit here."

I was in the middle of a hall; I couldn't see anything except directly ahead of me and directly behind me, and I couldn't see anything there. So I just began to backtrack; and when I got out into my living room I could look across my kitchen and standing on the outside of my house, at my sliding glass door was a demon spirit looking in.

It was a little dude; probably about four and a half foot high; sassy looking. You know how these bodybuilders develop their triceps muscles and all, and they get so big that they can't put their hands down like us little guys? They kind of have to stand with their arms angled out all the time because those muscles are so developed. They can force their hands in but it's not natural for them anymore.

Well that's the way that little maggot was standing. And it just reminded me of how I used to see boys standing when they were trying to be tough. He had his legs spread apart and he had those arms bowed out like: "Yeah, I'm bad."

Every hair on my body is still standing straight up. Now the Bible say: *"Submit yourselves therefore unto God. Resist the devil, and he will flee..."* Isn't that what it says? I had been submitted to God. I was in the presence of God. I'd been praying man; I mean the glory of God was all over me. And here I am standing face to face with this demon spirit.

The Spirit of the Lord said: "Rebuke him now and command him to leave." And there was some conversation between me and the Lord that I won't go into now; and finally the Lord spoke very sternly to me and He said: "I said rebuke him NOW." I said: "Yes Sir!" I pointed my finger at that spirit and I said: "In the name of Jesus Christ of Nazareth I take authority and dominion over you; and I command you to leave my home immediately, and do not return."

Guess what he did. He stood right there looking at me. I mean I hit that dude smooth on the chin with my best shot, and he just stood there. Do you know where I had come to? The battlefield of the mind; because now all of a sudden my mind is being flooded with thoughts. "It didn't work. You spoke the name of Jesus and he's still standing there; and he don't look like he's planning on leaving either."

It's amazing how many thoughts you can have zip through your mind in the matter of one second isn't it? I mean you can almost think your whole life; or it seems like it. It was too late to call the pastor on this one; I didn't have time.

The Bible says: *"Submit yourselves therefore unto God. Resist the devil, and he will flee from you."* That's all I knew. And I knew this: I did exactly what God told me to do. And then I knew this: There was nothing else I personally could do. I had declared the word of the Lord; I had invoked the power and the majesty of the name of Jesus; it's up to God now. Either He moves in on the scene, or boy I'm in big trouble.

"Resist the devil, and he will flee from you." With that little maggot still standing there looking at me I just turned and walked away just like: "That's it. I'm over you." I walked on down the hall; didn't look back; didn't even consider it; and before I got to the end of the hall all of my body hair laid back down; all those big ole goose bumps disappeared; and the Spirit of God in the sweetest voice you've ever heard said: "He's gone."

I didn't miss a step. I mean I went straight to the bed and as soon as I sat down and laid my head on the pillow: Boom! I was out.

The battlefield is in the mind. Don't you see that? I could have sat there; man I could have blew it big time. I could have messed that up big time and God only knows what kind of bondage and problems I would have allowed into my home.

See but I was renewing my mind and I was learning how to think the way God thinks so I could talk and act the way God talks and acts. And because of that I was able as a baby Christian; I hadn't been saved a month; I had not been born-again and Spirit filled for a month yet, but I was living in the Word. I was spending hours a day in the Word and in prayer; and I was able to stand face to face with a demon power and see him with my eyes, and walk out victorious over that situation. You can do the same thing. You can do the same thing but you have to make up your mind that you're going to do what it takes to get there. And that's get that old mind washed out with the Word of Almighty God; get it filled with God's Word; start talking God's talk; thinking God's thoughts; acting the way God acts; and you'll see the same power go to work for you that goes to work for God. And you can walk up to a situation that looks so hopeless; and you can say: "Let there be an abundance of finances released to fill this check book ledger in the name of Jesus."

When you get to a point where your mind is so renewed that you honestly believe in your heart that everything that you say is going to happen guess what; everything that you say is going to start happening. Not before; not before; but when you get there. And then you'll be that one that the Word talks about: "...and nothing shall be impossible to him that believes."

I don't know about you but I think it's worth going after. I'm purposing in my heart to dig in that much deeper, to study that much harder, to work this thing with every means available; because I don't know about you but I am not living in the 100fold realm that God would have me to live in. I know I'm not and it doesn't matter how much you've got you can't get all God has. There's more. There's more available. Do you hear me?

We need some people to rise up in the Body of Christ and absolutely take control of the financial realm. We need some Solomon's when it comes to the gold and the silver because we've got all kinds of work to do, and it costs big bucks.

"Well you know Brother if it was of God everything would just fall together; just fall in place. You wouldn't have to do anything." Barf. That is the stupidest; that's religion. That's religion; that's not the Word. The Word of God says that the devil is doing everything in his power to hinder, to steal it, to kill it, to choke the seed to death.

I'm going to tell you something, these guys that say: "I'm born-again; I'm Spirit filled; I'm a man of faith bless God, and I don't ever have any problems"; if they're not having problems I've strongly got to question whether or not they're even saved.

I don't believe in preaching a negative gospel. I believe in preaching truth. Jesus promised us: *"In the world ye shall have tribulation"* (Jn. 16:33). *"Many are the afflictions of the righteous: but the Lord delivereth him out of them all"* (Ps. 34:19). Hallelujah.

So this ole bunch that comes along; these ole hyper-faiths; these ole super Christians you know, that just because you have problems say: "They don't know how to exercise faith and live by faith" and they don't ever have any problems; they're liars. And don't you let them bring condemnation on you because you're having problems. Why would you even need faith if you didn't have a battle to win? How can you have victory without a battle?

So let's forget this ole religious junk that has rotted our thinking, and robbed us of the blessings of God; and let's renew our minds to the Word of God; and start thinking the way God thinks; and talking that way; and acting as if it's so. And bless God, it will be.

Chapter 4

I want to start this chapter off by looking at II Corinthians 10. You probably quote these Scriptures. If not, you've probably heard it preached on about a thousand eight hundred and sixty-two times. But the Bible says we need to rehearse these things regularly.

"For though we walk in the flesh, we do not war after the flesh:"

Our warfare is not natural. He goes on to say:

"(For the weapons of our warfare are *not carnal,"*

They are not earthy; they are not of the flesh; they are not of the world. We don't have to rely on the strong arm of the flesh. Thank God that through the faith of Jesus Christ of Nazareth I believe that we can walk in perfect safety even through the valley of shadow of death we do not have to fear evil. We do not have to fear some fool coming and knocking us over the head; even if he comes up and starts roaring against us as a lion.

We can invoke the power and the majesty of the awesome name of Jesus. And I believe that you're going to hear in the days to come; I'm going to give you this by the Spirit of Revelation; in the days to come you're going to start hearing about saints of God who have uttered the name of Jesus in the face of muggers, and even as it was in the days that they came to take Jesus and He said: "Whom seek ye?"; and they said: "We seek Jesus" and He opened His mouth and said: "I am"; and they were driven back and fell to their faces because of the power of God. You're going to see it come to pass in this day and in this hour. Mark it down. Hallelujah.

We don't have to rely on guns and knives. We've got the Word of Almighty God and the name of Jesus. It goes on to say:

"...but mighty through God to the pulling down of strong holds;)

Casting down imaginations, and every high thing that exalteth itself against the knowledge of God, and bringing into captivity every thought to the obedience of Christ;" (Vs.3-5).

I want you to notice first of all that Scripture said that thoughts would be there that had to be taken captive. I'm sick and tired of the devil convincing people that they've sinned because they've had an evil thought. It is not sin to have evil thoughts. Let me repeat it: It is not sin to have an evil thought. You can't keep them out. You cannot keep them out. I don't care how holy you are.

You've got an enemy and he's got the ability to fire fiery darts into your thought life. To have the thought is not sin. It's what you do with it that determines whether it becomes sin or not. Do you hear what I'm preaching? This is good.

It's not the thought that's sin; it's what's done with the thought that determines whether or not it becomes sin; or you continue to victory and glorious power.

The Bible said that these demonic strong holds are

built into our minds. They gain entrance through our thoughts. But through the power of God and the grace of God we are able to bring them into captivity. Now a thought meditated upon becomes an imagination. An imagination not dealt with creates vision. That's literally what a vision of the heart is.

God builds strong holds inside of you and me. See we've heard so much preaching about tearing down strong holds that we've kind of gotten the mistaken idea that every strong hold is bad. Not so. We ought to be constantly creating new strong holds in our lives every single day; but, they should be godly strong holds from the Word of Almighty God.

The word "strong" hold in the Greek is **ŏchurōma** (okh-oo'-ro-mah)[ii]. It means a fortress or to make firm. We ought to make God's Word **firm** in our hearts and minds that it becomes a literal fortress unto us; no way that the enemy can get beyond the gate. Amen? He can get up to the gate but he's going to bounce off when he hits it.

I'm glad on the other hand to know that the gates of hell shall <u>not</u> prevail against me (Matt. 16:18). Did you hear what I said? The gates of hell shall not prevail against ME. Say that.

See, we thought Jesus was talking defensibly when He said that. "You know, when the devil comes against ya, uh, you won't knuckle under and fold." That's not what He was talking about at all.

People say: "We've got to stay away from that militant Christianity." That's what we've got to get to. Jesus was the most militant dude that walked the earth.

He went looking for a good fight. Hallelujah; but He didn't fight with man. He recognized the true enemy and He went after him.

The gates of hell shall not prevail. We ought to be getting up on a daily basis storming those gates; attacking those gates; aggressively tearing those gates down and going into the very bowels and heart of hell, and bringing the captives out. That's exactly what He was talking about.

The Word of God can become a fortress. It can become a strong hold; but, there is also the negative side of that; that when those thoughts come in you must deal with those thoughts because if you don't, and you continue to think along those lines you form an imagination. An imagination creates a vision on the inside of you; and the next thing you know you're doing; you're acting out the vision.

Did you ever wonder why so many violent crimes were connected with movies that people were watching? I heard Pat Robertson one day reporting on crimes of rape and sexual crimes. He said about 90% of all those that commit those crimes they have found out through studies and interrogations, and questioning; about 90% of those people are heavily involved in pornography.

Thoughts, imaginations, visions of the heart, actions. Do you think this is a game? You better back up and re-look at it. It's not a game. It's not innocent. It's not some little ole light thing you know, that we just: "Well that was a good little ole word Brother." And then you go off and go: "How could this possibly..." Mark it. Mark it. Mark it. This is real. This is real; thank God for

His truth.

Look at I Peter 1:13. I'm going to show you something that may shock you and it's going to answer some questions for you about people who are in false religions.

"Wherefore gird up the loins of your mind, be sober, and hope to the end for the grace that is to be brought unto you at the revelation of Jesus Christ;"

That word "loins" in the Greek is **ŏsphus** (os-foos')[iii]. It literally means creative power.

"Wherefore bind up the creative power of your mind..." There is a thing called psychic power and it comes from the soul. The human mind has creative power. I'll tell you one thing that it creates that you've probably never even stopped to consider: Emotion.

Did you know that your thoughts will create an emotion? Your thoughts have the power to create emotion. I can create anger any time I want to. So can you. All I have to do is start thinking about things that aggravate, and annoy, and make me mad. And all of a sudden an emotion; a mood; maybe it makes more sense to you that way; a mood will come over me. The next thing you know if I don't deal with that mood I've punched a hole in a wall, or gotten into a fight with somebody.

You know you can get in a fight at church. Probably some of the worse fights you'll ever get in will be at church; some churches. You can get anything that you're looking for. You can create it. And you know the Christian always wants to blame somebody else.

"The devil made me do that. Look what the devil's doing to me." Isn't that our scapegoat; blame everything on the devil that we don't like? Most of the time he's not within a country mile. We're creating our own situations; our own moods; our own emotions.

The husband asks the wife something; she's been running around behind kids all day screaming and hollering; tearing everything in the house apart that they possibly can bless their darling little angel hearts. Except for of course I had perfect children; and those of you that don't have any yet, just wait. Yours' will be perfect too; they'll be as "perfect" as mine were.

And she's been feeling bad. The old devil has been attacking her in her body and she's been trying to stand on the Word for that; and she's been running around cleaning up spills, and messes, and this, and that, and the other; and the husband comes in and says: "What's for supper?" And she says: "I don't know! I haven't had a chance to think about it!" And immediately he goes: "Humph! Who do you think you are? Bless God I'll tell you one thing: I'm the king of this place!" Hello? "You better git yo'self into subjection heah! Submit yo'self woman!"

And boy then we go tooth, hair and nail; amen? You see, words only have power over you if you allow them to. Do you hear what I'm saying? Do you know what the Bible says about a soft word? It turns away wrath. Amen. Let's grow up husbands. Let's grow up wives. Come on mom and dad let's get it right.

The mind has creative power and it can create imaginations; it can create vanities, things that are vain; it can create godly things; and here's the part about it; it's just natural for it to do that so most of us never really stop to even consider it, and listen to me, it is a power that can be controlled and focused.

In martial arts you can take a person who comes in and attacks and you can block; and there are techniques that use an open hand. Say a guy comes in and throws an attack and let's say I block it. I can take an open hand and hit him in the ribs; and what it does is that it not only stops him but it jars everything in him. But if I took the same speed, and the same power, and I hit him with one little, bitty point the damage is much greater. Why? It's because the power is focused.

The mind has creative power. It must be controlled and focused so that it can do the absolute, ultimate damage to the kingdom of the devil. Now that's why God put that in there. And another reason He put it in there is because He has it. He does; because you're created just like Him; in the same image and likeness as God Almighty.

People think anger is a bad thing. It's not, if it's focused; if it's controlled and focused. We should be angry about abortion but we shouldn't go blow up abortion clinics. We shouldn't drive by and you know, pop a cap at the people that are trying to get in the door. Amen? That's destructive; that's uncontrolled.

We need to take the creative power of God, the grace of God, the faith of God and focus it to get things changed on planet Earth.

Well, the Bible says in Romans 8:37 that we're more than conquerors through Him that loved us. That word "conquerors" is a Greek word that means to vanquish beyond, to gain a decisive victory. I like that. You know it's not: "Boy I just barely did win that one." Uh ah; do you hear what I'm saying? To gain a <u>decisive</u> victory; to vanquish beyond.

That word "vanquish"; I looked up in the Webster's Dictionary. And to vanquish means to overcome in battle or in a contest; listen to this; to gain mastery over as an emotion.

"I can't help it! I've always had a bad temper bless God! My daddy had it! My granddaddy had it! I guess I'll always have it!" If you want it you can; but don't you sit there and insult my intelligence, and tell me there's nothing that you can do about it. I know. I don't think there was anybody more violent natured than I was. Look at me wrong. Or, let me think you're looking at me wrong.

Thank God I got over that. I renewed my mind. I built a different kind of a strong hold in there. I tore the one out that was there and I put a new one in its place. That's what you have to do. As you remove these demonic strong holds if you don't replace it with a godly strong hold that ole dirty thing will come right back in. And it'll re-root itself; and it'll bring some neighbours, friends and relatives with it.

You remember Jesus' teaching where He said when an unclean spirit goes out of a man he goes into <u>dry</u> places seeking some comfort, and some rest; but he can't find any so he says to himself: "I'll go back to my house that I came out of." What was he talking about: "his house"?

You're living inside a house. You call it a body. You're a spirit; and you live in a house called a body. The Greek is **soma**; it means slave. Your body is supposed to obey you not vice versa. That's why we have so much carnality in the Church because Christians never learn to get that flesh under subjection because they haven't renewed their minds; and they're losing it on the battlefield of the mind. Their flesh dictates to them what they do or don't do.

"I wish that preacher would shut up. I'll tell you the truth; I can't sit there for an hour and listen to the Word of God." You poor, pitiful thing. Why don't you go wait out in the car and hold your wife's purse in the process? That's the truth; you might as well amen me, you know it is.

Your body is a slave. You control that flesh. "Brother I'll tell you one thing: I can't help it. I've just got to eat everything I see." Don't you lie to me. Quit lying to yourself. You do not have to eat everything you see; unless you're body ruled. And if you're body ruled you'll never amount to a hill of beans in the Kingdom of Heaven. Amen!

It's time to grow up in this stuff and quit fooling ourselves; and playing stupid little ole religious games with ourselves. People are dying out there and going to hell; and we're playing these stupid little games. We're going to tell them that God loves them and He's all powerful; and they look at our life and say: "Well why don't you quit? How come He don't meet some of your needs?"

Now if you want to preach that ole junk that says:

"Well you know, Brother, Sister, you may have to live like a pauper and a beggar down here, but there's a better home in glory waitin for ya. You know, you can get saved, and at least in all your misery you can have God's peace. At least in all your sufferin you'll know that when you get on the other side you'll have a better place."

If you want to preach that junk go somewhere else. I'm not going to live that way. I'm not going to preach that way. I'm not going to teach that way. I'm not going to pray and prophesy that way. I'm going to live according to the Word. Hallelujah.

And the Word says we can gain the mastery over our lives; every area of our lives; but it's going to take some work. It's not going to just automatically happen as Brother Hagin used to say: "It's not going to just fall out of the sky like ripe cherries on us." It's going to take a made up mind.

Do you know how I got off Parris Island? My mind was made up. Did you know I proved this without the Holy Ghost; not even having the knowledge it was in God's Word; I proved this as an unregenerate, lost sinner that the mind has creative power.

Those drill instructors sixteen hours a day constantly beat and badgered us, and told us: "You'll never make it off this rock. You will not make it. We're gonna kill you; we're gonna break you; we're gonna drive you nuts; you ain't gettin off. You scum suckin dogs; you don't deserve the title Marine! You'll never get it."

I had a made up mind. I said: "Yes I will. They may carry me out of here in a box but I'm goin off this rock one way or the other; and in the mean while you keep dishin. I'm gonna take it." And they did. And I did! Fourteen out of 90 men graduated when we were supposed to.

Even in the natural it works. Now what you reckon we can do with this filled with the Holy Ghost; the creative Agent of God inside of us working with what is already there in the natural? Good Lord, there can be no stopping us.

We don't have to stay with the quality of life that we presently have if we're not satisfied with it. We created it. You created exactly the situation you're in right now. You did that; and because you created it that means you have the ability to re-create something different. Hallelujah; I like that. You see, that's good news.

Well we see that we can become; we can vanquish beyond; we can gain the decisive victory praise God. But I'd put you in remembrance of Joshua 24:15 that says: *"Choose ye this day whom ye will serve;"*

The choice is up to you. That's why I told you about that boot camp thing. It doesn't matter what other people tell you. It doesn't matter if everybody in your world is coming down on your head and shoulders. It doesn't matter if they're jumping on you with both feet. It doesn't matter what demons and devils tell you. The choice is up to you.

You decide who you're going to serve; who you're going to believe; who you're going to agree with. Are you going to agree with all of those negative talkers? You know one thing about people is that they're so jealous; even Christians. And when they see God start using you immediately they start criticizing. "Who does he think he is? I know where he lives. I saw him whip his kid the other day." Thank God, you saw him doing the Word. If you love your kid you're going to do whatever you have to do to get his attention. That means if you've got to ground them; you've got to pull their driver's license or quit paying their insurance; that means you've got to restrict them and don't let them go out for weeks at a time. You let them bawl and squall, and balk and complain, and gripe and moan; let them do it; it's not going to hurt you and it's going to develop some character in their life; and it's going to teach them some responsibility.

Is it easy? No. I used to hear that ole saying: "Son this hurts me more than it does you" and I said: "Yeah." On the receiving end they can't understand that. They don't even believe it. But when I got to be a daddy I found out it really is true. It hurt me a whole lot more than my kids to have to punish them because I didn't want to have to punish them. I wanted them to be good. I wanted them to do right. Every momma and daddy wants that for their kids.

But the Word of God says that if we love them we'll switch them legs when they need it. The rod of correction will drive folly far from the child (Prov. 22:15). I found that always worked in my case. We used to try and hide my dad's belt. I know he had revelation knowledge working in his life. There wasn't anywhere that we could hide that thing that he couldn't find. And boy when he did.

Moving right along; let's look at Deuteronomy

30. I love this portion of Scripture here. This makes it so clear what I've been telling you about choice and about other people not being able to hold you down or hold you back, even if they have set themselves against you deliberately.

You know promotion comes from God not from man; and I've proven this time and time and time in my life because in spite of natural conditions and situations I've just agreed with God's Word and I've seen it cause people that didn't even like me turn and change, and turn around and bless me.

"I call heaven and earth to record this day against you, that *I have set before you life and death, blessing and cursing: therefore choose life, that both thou and thy seed may live:"* (Vs. 19).

We affect the lives of our children even by the choices and the decisions we make and by the way we live our life. They say that most wife abusers; they say that almost all child molesters are people who were molested when they were children. Do you see how serious this is? Do you see how powerful this is?

The Bible says that God will visit the iniquity of the father's to the children to the third and the fourth generation (Ex. 34:7). Do you know what? When you do not honor God's Word you have set yourself against God. You will lose. And here's the sad part: It may affect your children for the rest of their lives. You see not doing it God's way will always cost you more than you want to pay.

II Corinthians 1:20 says –

"For all the promises of God in him are *yea, and in him Amen, unto the glory of God by us."*

The choice is up to us. We say; we make the decisions not the devil, and not those who are around you.

Now let's look at Philippians 2:5 –

Let *this mind be in you, which was also in Christ Jesus:"*

Have you ever noticed that before? You have a choice. "Ooh; are you telling me I can have the same mind that's in Christ Jesus?" Yes that's exactly what I'm telling you because that's what God's Word just said. As a matter of fact, over in I Corinthians the Bible says *"we have the mind of Christ"* (2:16).

Does that mean when we get over in the sweet by and by we'll come into this? Uh ah; he says we have the mind of Christ. However, we must LET that mind be in us. How do we let it? We renew our mind. Remember that word "renew" in the Greek means to rejuvenate. We re-train our thinking process.

You were trained how to think. A lot of elements contributed to it; public schools or private schools, or home schools, or whatever. You've been trained to a large extent how to think. Well if you were trained once you can be re-trained. But you have to make up your mind that you're going to do it.

Anybody who has studied, taken any kind of courses at home, been involved in any kind of correspondence school or online school; you know it's tough. It's a whole lot easier to go sit in a classroom and listen to a teacher, or a professor, or whatever just lecture and take notes; and have the advantage of having the open forum when you get into class discussions and you hear the thoughts, and the views, and the questions, and the things of those other students. Man that's the best way in the world to learn. It's the easiest way. I'll put it that way. It may not be the best but it's the easiest.

But when you start doing self study it's tough. It's hard. But, it's possible; but it takes discipline. You have to control your life and your priorities; and you have to manage your time wisely. You have to be a good steward with your time. Most people do not manage any of their time. They just literally run from this place to that place just kind of reacting and responding. They put out this fire and then that fire; and then go to the next fire. And they say: "Boy when I can get this fire put out I can sit down and rest" but they can't ever sit down and rest because the devil makes sure there's always a new fire.

You have to sit down and write down everything that you have to do. Write down the things you HAVE to do; and then things you NEED to do come next. And you write down: How long does it take to do these things? How much is left? What can I cut out? What can I move to a lower level of priority that I insert this in its place?

You have to do that. It doesn't just come to you in a dream one night. It's just not going to happen. You have to take control of your life rather than letting your life control you. And if you don't renew your mind you never will.

It comes through your wilful, deliberate application of God's Word in your life. I'm talking about the mind of Christ. The Bible is the written Word of God; Jesus is the living Word. The Bible is God's mind. The Bible is a part of God's mind that has been revealed to man; and we can get it in us. We can let it be in there and we can let it rule, and reign, and dominate, and lead, and guide our life. And when we do we'll always see the power that Jesus walked in flowing through our lives.

Why should we? I mean if I can just get saved and go to heaven when I die; do the best I can while I'm here; why should I? I want to show you a couple of places in Scripture.

"Now the Spirit speaketh expressly, that in the latter times some shall depart from the faith, giving heed to seducing spirits, and doctrines of devils.

Speaking lies in hypocrisy; having their conscience seared with a hot iron;" (I Tim. 4:1-2).

That word "seared" is **kautēriazō** (kow-tay-ree-ad'-zō)[iv] and means to burn in with a branding iron, branded, or cauterized. We cauterize wounds sometimes so that it won't get infected but what happens is it kills the flesh. After having been in the faith you can have your conscience become seared. I don't think anybody reading this book wants that.

Seducing spirits are constantly trying to pull you away from the faith of God; to pull you off God's Word. So this is one of the areas you say: Why not do it? Because you run the high risk and the possibility of having the devil cause your conscience to become seared against the things of God; totally dead so that there's no way that you can receive from God.

Let's look back at Genesis 3. We see the curse being introduced.

"Unto the woman he said, I will greatly multiply thy sorrow and thy conception; in sorrow thou shalt bring forth children; and thy desire shall be *to thy husband, and he shall rule over thee.*

And unto Adam he said, Because thou hast hearkened unto the voice of thy wife, and hast eaten of the tree, of which I commanded thee, saying, Thou shalt not eat of it: cursed is *the ground for thy sake; in sorrow shalt thou eat* of *it all the days of thy life;"* (Vs. 16-17).

By not renewing your mind with God's Word, and keeping your mind renewed, and controlling your thought life which also dictates what your words and your actions will be, you are going to greatly increase your sorrow and hardship in the here and now. Unless you're just a masochist, and if you are I can cast it out of you, only a masochist enjoys sorrow, and pain, and hardship. That's not saying that we don't learn how to endure it because we certainly do; but that doesn't mean we enjoy it because we have a "right" mind not a wrong mind, or a corrupted mind.

So we see that these people that bawl and squall, and moan and groan when you start talking to them and asking them how much time they spend in the Word everyday; how much time they spend with the Lord in prayer and you come to find out maybe three to five, six to seven minutes a day; and they can't figure out why it isn't working; had you ever wondered how their sorrow always seemed to be so great? And if you want to be just like them you can. The choice is yours. But if not you're going to have to make up your mind that you're going to do what it takes to change things.

I told you that you have to do it. You have to deal with your soul after you get born-again because the born-again experience just deals with the spirit of man. You begin to renew the mind; you start dealing with your soulish realm so that you can gain mastery over the body; and now the tri-unity of yourself once you get there, will be flowing, and functioning, and operating like Jesus.

I showed you the need for it. I showed you that the choice is yours. I showed you what will happen if you don't do it. I'd be doing you an injustice if I stopped now because I haven't told you how to do it. How do we renew our mind and walk in this victory day by day?

"This book of the law shall not depart out of thy mouth; but thou shalt <u>meditate</u> therein <u>day and night</u>, that thou mayest <u>observe to do</u> according to all that is written therein: <u>for then</u> <u>thou</u> shalt make thy way prosperous, and then thou shalt have good success" (Josh. 1:8).

That word "meditate" in the Hebrew not only means to think about and consider it but it also means: to mutter to oneself. Let this word not depart out of your mouth but mutter it to yourself. Keep speaking God's Word continuously; and do it to yourself as well as to the mountain; as well as to the sycamore tree; as well as to the fig tree. Faith cometh by hearing it.

You are going to make your way prosperous. Did you hear that? Then and only then will you be prosperous and have good success; not before.

Let's go back to I Timothy chapter 4.

"Till I come, <u>give attendance to</u> reading, to exhortation, to doctrine.

Neglect not the gift that is in thee, which was given thee by prophecy, with the laying on of the hands of the presbytery.

<u>Meditate</u> upon these things; give thyself <u>wholly</u> to them;"

There's that word "meditate" again. He didn't say give thyself a little bit to them; you know, casually or occasionally. "Well you know Brother, I'm afraid you've gone off the deep end. You know there is such a thing as "too much". Give thyself wholly, completely, totally to them.

"...that thy profiting may appear to all."

"Well you know we have to have variety."

"...give thyself wholly to them; that thy profiting may appear to all.

Take heed unto thyself, and unto the doctrine;"

Take heed to the devil? I mean after all, doesn't he run the show? Not hardly.

"Take heed unto <u>thyself</u>, and unto the doctrine..."

You could say: unto the Word.

"...continue in them: for in doing this thou shalt both save <u>thyself</u>, <u>and them</u> that hear thee" (Vs. 13-16).

<u>If</u> they'll do what you tell them. See I can't make you prosperous and I can't make you successful. And I can't make you a great man or woman of faith. All I can do is teach and preach these things that are becoming of

sound doctrine. YOU have to give heed unto yourself.

Lastly, let's read Philippians 4:4-9 from the Amplified New Testament. This tells us how; how to renew our minds and how to control our life, and our thoughts and our actions.

"Rejoice in the Lord" whenever you feel good; "always"; I might add this: Especially when you don't feel good.

"Rejoice in the Lord always – delight, gladden <u>*yourselves*</u> *in Him..."*

Gladden <u>yourself</u>. That just keeps popping up everywhere I turn to in the Book.

"...again I say, Rejoice!

Do not fret or *have any anxiety about anything,* but *in every circumstance and in everything by prayer and petition [definite requests] with thanksgiving continue to make your wants known to God.*

And God's peace [be yours, that tranquil state of a soul assured of its salvation through Christ, and so fearing nothing from God and content with its earthly lot of whatever sort that is, that peace] which transcends all understanding, shall garrison and *mount guard over your hearts and minds in Christ Jesus.*

For the rest, brethren, whatever is true, whatever is worthy of reverence and *is honourable* and *seemly, whatever is just, whatever is pure, whatever is lovely* and *lovable, whatever is kind* and *winsome* and *gracious, if there is any virtue* and *excellence, if there is anything worthy of praise, <u>think on</u>* and *<u>weigh</u>* and *<u>take account of</u> these things --- <u>fix your minds</u> on them."*

The battlefield beloved is the mind. Even when it comes in our bodies you'll find that instantly your mind is being bombarded as well. You can change the situation in your body. You can change the situation in your home; in your marriage; in your family; in your business; in your finances; in your relationships; on your job.

You can renew your mind and you should do it on a daily basis. You take control of your life. Don't let ole slough foot do it. You can do it. I can't do it for you. You've got to do it for yourself. Purpose in your heart today to do just that.

---

[i] James Strong, LL.D., S.T.D., *The New Strong's Exhaustive Concordance of the Bible*, Thomas Nelson Publishers, Nashville, Camden, New York, *Greek Dictionary of the New Testament*, #4995, 70

[ii] Ibid, #3794, 53
[iii] Ibid, #3751, 53
[iv] Ibid, #2743, 41

Made in the USA
Middletown, DE
22 May 2022

66086453R00047